Work.

Curse or blessing? The deception of the system. Learning to move from a job, through a career, to your work.

GP
GloriPub

Work. Curse or Blessing?
The deception of the system.
Learning to move from a job, through a career, to your work.
Published by Gloripub
http://www.gloripub.com
Printed in the U.S.A
The Kingdom Team

Request for information should be addressed to:
http://www.gloripub.com
http://www.thekingdomteam.com
http://www.davidsampong.space
Instagram/twitter: @dsashun
YouTube: David Sampong

ISBN-13: 978-0-9976213-1-0
ISBN-10: 0-9976213-1-1

Contents

DEDICATION

To the King of the kingdom of God and His Governor.
To all who are fed up with the system.
To all who want to find and understand their work and purpose.
To all who have been set free by the power of God and have been welcomed back into the kingdom of heaven.

ACKNOWLEDGEMENT

To my parents and siblings, my wonderful wife, Jemimah and Philip Asmah whose words sparked the revolution of my writings.

"For it will be like a man going on a journey, who called his servants and entrusted to them his property. To one he gave five talents, to another two, to another one, to each according to his ability. Then he went away. He who had received the five talents went at once and traded with them, and he made five talents more. So also he who had the two talents made two talents more. But he who had received the one talent went and dug in the ground and hid his master's money. Now after a long time, the master of those servants came and settled accounts with them. And he who had received the five talents came forward, bringing five talents more, saying, 'Master, you delivered to me five talents; here I have made five talents more.' His master said to him, 'Well done, good and faithful servant. You have been faithful over a little; I will set you over much. Enter into the joy of your master.' And he also who had the two talents came forward, saying, 'Master, you delivered to me two talents; here I have made two talents more.' His master said to him, 'Well done, good and faithful servant. You have been faithful over a little; I will set you over much. Enter into the joy of your master.' He also who had received the one talent came forward, saying, 'Master, I knew you to be a hard man, reaping where you did not sow, and gathering where you scattered no seed, so I was afraid, and I went and hid your talent in the ground. Here you have what is yours.' But his master answered him, 'You wicked and slothful servant! You knew that I reap where I have not sown and gather where I scattered no seed? Then you ought to have invested my money with the bankers, and at my coming I should have received what was my own with interest. So take the talent from him and give it to him who has the ten talents. For to everyone who has will more be given, and he will have an abundance. But from the one who has not, even what he has will be taken away. And cast the worthless servant into the outer darkness. In that place, there will be weeping and gnashing of teeth.'
-- Matthew 25:14-25

FOREWORD

Work examines the concept of having a job, career or any form of employment as a journey. It looks at the nuances of this journey and takes you on not only a personal, but also a spiritual ride that illustrates what the differences between each stage is. It also elaborates on God's role in one's employment life, and using biblical quotes, paints a vivid picture of how God not only tests us, but also gives us a chance to be happy. David shares anecdotes of his life, as well as famous quotes to create a cohesive message about a subject not many people bother to think about, let alone analyze. It is a riveting and essential read about happiness and comfort, and David is the perfect scribe to take on this narrative.

- Clifford Owusu
Comedian/ YouTube Sensation

PREFACE

I have had the opportunity of working at three great companies in the United States, all located in New York City. I loved the fact that I could tell people I worked at a prominent place and see a sense of validation on their faces, which was conveyed via their smiles. This was a prideful thing to do, but deep within me, I never saw it that way. I thought the more I let people know where I work, the more information I give them about how successful I have become. God has a way of humbling a human being that sometimes we as humans cannot understand. To me, this was my source of income; I was very excited to be working for these companies, money coming in every day from every angle. This is what many people are going through now—they are working two to three jobs', thinking it helps pay the bills, while others think that it is their source of income to the point that they put their all into it. I am not saying you should not put your all, but as you do, do not make it your source. In my case, since that was my supposed source of income, I became prideful. As I stated before, God has a unique way of humbling us. As I was working at these three jobs, I got a job offer from the city which was a big break at the time. This had everything to do with the career path I was taking. I went in for the interview, and the interview went great. About a week after, I was told I had the job and was given a start date and where to report. Bear in mind that this paid better than all the other three jobs combined so with that in mind, I put in my resignation letter at all three jobs. In a matter of one week, I had let go of three great jobs for one big career; little did I know that I was being set up by God.

Monday morning, my start date for my new job came, so I reported to work bright and early. When I got in, there was no one there so I had to wait. After about fifteen minutes, the big boss came in (this was the person who interviewed me and he knew my name). The first thing he asked was, "David what are you doing here this morning?" To my amazement, I answered that I was told that my start date was that morning and that I was also to report to work there. This is where things turned interesting; he informed me that I wasn't supposed to be there and that I should have received an email letting me know that there is a hiring freeze in the city and that affected me also. To my shock, I started to think about the jobs I had just let go of. I didn't want to leave the office because now I had nowhere to go but home. I eventually had to leave, in my disappointment. I took the bus and kept thinking about what had just happened. Now I have no job, I have to pay rent and all the other bills that came along with it. I was humbled; I had no hope anywhere now but in God alone, and suddenly, He became my source. I applied for many jobs but no calls came through, I spent most of my time in the church and at home, that was my daily routine for a while. After about two months of being without a job, I received an email to reply stating "I accept" to a job offer that I never applied for, moreover, the salary was about twice that of what I would have made if there was no hiring freeze. After working at the career for about five years, I felt uncomfortable because I couldn't understand why, I, as a person sent to this earth, was stuck at a 9-5 job as we call it. I had to dig deep within myself and see what I was capable of doing and who I really was. The most important question came to mind, the question of "why am I here?" Once I was able to figure that out, I realized it was time to move past this career phase.

I started off at a job, but as much as I liked the job, I realized that there was no real satisfaction in it. How can one be working at three great places, spending most of his or her time there, yet cannot make ends meet? The urge to be better moved me to get an education and this helped with the career I got in the story. At the career, I learned a lot of things and this helped me in life; it was also at this career that I found my work. This work was fulfilling, and the difference between what I did at the job and my previous jobs was very clear. It is important to understand the essence of work. This concept gave birth to this book. My sincere hope is that the lessons herein will benefit all who read this book, and also those who are ready to leave their jobs and career and embark on a journey to find their work.

INTRODUCTION

I always thought these three words meant the same thing: job, career, and work. We often interchange them thinking they are the same. Many things we do are overlooked and that goes even for the way we refer to things. For instance, instead of calling our offspring, children, we call them kids thinking it is the same thing. That is what we see with the words listed. I, for one, thought the words "job" and "career" were interchangeable until I came to understand that there was one other word that we completely overlook or don't think about—WORK, or we think it's merely what we do in order to put food on the table. Many of us urge people to quit a job and pursue a career, but that's as far as it goes. I do not blame them anyway because that's what they have also been taught. If you are very smart but learn the wrong thing, you will be a smart person with wrong information. The system and the world we live in has dictated what we have to believe and this has been embedded in our mind and even our subconscious. It takes the grace of God to free us from this mental bondage. We have to start doing something that many are not doing. We have to start *thinking differently.* As mentioned earlier, a countless number of people think work is what you do to put food on the table and to clothe oneself. Others think a job only helps pay the monthly bills—basically, it helps maintain the standard of living one enjoys. Finally, a career is the prize winner, and achieving that deems one successful. Most educated individuals think that their career is what makes them wealthy and that is what our parents even taught us while we were growing up. This is a notion I will like to erase from the minds of many individuals. This is what motivated the writing of this book. Many are stuck in this mental bondage and the knowledge in this book, I believe, will set them free by the power of God. In this book, I tackle what a job is, the importance of a job, what it entails and what one supposedly does at a job. With the understanding of that, we dive into a career by first comparing it to a job, defining it and understanding what the middle class is all about. And finally, we talk about work by first understanding what it is, and conclude by examining whether it's a curse or a blessing, We look at what Jesus thought about work and how we ought to even embark on accomplishing that—it goes beyond our notion of making that money to pay that bill. Finally, we'll bring to light the true meaning of *success* as we embark on being set free mentally.

In each chapter, we will examine what each of the three phases is by understanding the role and purpose for each of them. Once we know what each stage is, we will look at some biblical figures and see how they embraced each phase. Finally, we will look at the lessons we are supposed to learn from each phase.

Job training empowers people to realize their dreams and improve their lives.
-- Sylvia Mathews Burwell

1

JOB

And he said, "There was a man who had two sons. And the younger of them said to his father, 'Father, give me the share of property that is coming to me.' And he divided his property between them. Not many days later, the younger son gathered all he had and took a journey into a far country, and there he squandered his property in reckless living.

-- Luke 15:11-13

In life we always have to start from somewhere to get to where we were purposed to be or where we imagine ourselves. Not many of us are born with a silver spoon in our mouth. If you are like many of us, you were not born in the richest family in the world, or even born into a family that already had all that you wanted. In this world, very few people are given that privilege, while others have to pursue that dream. Many strive to greatness without even knowing that they are striving, but when they get there they are happy about the journey. At a point in every child's life, they will want to do some kind of job that will bring in some type of income. This is usually around the teenage age, where most want their freedom. Little do they know that this is the beginning of bondage.

As stated before, not many of us are born into rich families, so taking on a job is the only way a fifteen-year-old boy thinks he can help the family out (that is if they have that mindset). Others think it is the only way they can get what they truly want. Before we can even talk about the fifteen-year-old teenager, let us consider the parents, are they in a job themselves or are they in a career? A growing trend I have noticed is that many people, especially uneducated people, often focus on getting a new job always. When they find a job that will pay them better than where they are currently working, they leave their current job to the better job. Because many parents are doing that, their children think that is the way of life, and they then start to follow that same pursuit. What then is a job? Well, Merriam Webster defines it as "something that a person does regularly in order to earn money". We often like to talk about jobs and career. Very few people actually pursue a career. Many, on the other hand, like to stick to the job they have.

From a survey I conducted, I realized that people usually stick to the job they have because of the little discounts they get at their job place or are just satisfied with what they are doing. Others, on the other hand, do not think anything better of themselves. They will rather get up in the morning, go into a job they hate, and clock in for a period of time for the little money that is offered to them. Many people do not understand the essence of a job anyway, which is why they keep themselves in a job for years. I worked at a retail store, and I was surprised to see people that I had worked with who had been at that job for years. One of my coworkers had worked there for about fifty-one years, after which she retired from the job. Immediately she retired, she passed away. Another guy had also worked at the place for over twenty years doing the same thing—cutting boxes. If you will stay at a job for that many years, I believe you should aim to at least become a manager. But to stay in that position for years, that tells us something. I realized that some of them were comfortable with the money they were making and didn't feel the need to even consider other ventures.

The gentleman who had worked there for over twenty-five years was making about the same salary as a manager who recently started, and this made him feel that there was no point pursuing that position. The crazy thing was that whenever there was no manager around, he was put in charge because he had seniority. I believe that this should have been a wakeup call, but that never happened. We have either let low self-esteem keep us down for so long that we never see ourselves past the jobs we are working at or we just get set in that comfort zone.

A growing trend I see among people who migrate from other countries to the west is that the first thing they seek is a job. This is not a bad thing, the only thing is that once they get there, they get comfortable, especially when the money starts flowing. The currency difference makes them think the little money they make is big enough until they fully understand the system. Many people migrate to the United States and immediately become a home health aide, a certified nursing assistant, sales associate or other low earning jobs and stop right there. Others do these jobs and go to school at the same time, while supporting family back home. Many just stay and enjoy the life they live in.

Many like myself come and get into the retail sector. Some stay there because they get a store discount to shop so they refuse to leave. When I first came to the United States, my father taught me the system and then together with my auntie, they helped get me a job at a well-renowned retail store. For starters, I was excited to work there. The name alone made me want to work there. The more I worked there, I kept picking up certain information to better myself. It was there that I met the coworkers who had been working there for over twenty years. That made me question myself. I kept asking myself a question, the same question I want everyone who has a job to ask themselves, "**Is this what I want to be doing for the rest of my life?**" This is the question most people never ask themselves while growing up. When I asked some of my coworkers at the time, they said it was too late. It is never too late to start anything. It takes a changed mindset to move past current situations. Once I realized that that was not what I wanted, I started making moves to better myself. **Whenever you make an effort to leave your job, God makes sure that He backs you up with the necessary provisions to help you out in ways you cannot phantom.** We will talk more about this in the next chapter.

If you have read my book *"From Bondage to Freedom"*, you will understand a little bit about what the job phase is. The job phase of every human being's life is the deliverance stage. Why do I say that? This is because it is at this point that one knows that they need to move up in life. Many people who are in the deliverance stage usually think that it is freedom. This applies to some people in the job phase as well. The job phase should be the stepping stone to get one to the career phase which we will be talking about in the next chapter. One thing most people do not think about is the fact that as long as they are working at a job, they will always be at the bottom of the economic ladder.

> *There are three types of people. There are those like you who come and eat here, those who work here for minimum wage and those who own this place. If you want to be wealthy, you want to be an owner*
>
> *--David Bach*

Let's take the retail store I worked at for instance. This was one of the things that motivated me to get out of the job phase. Every Thanksgiving Day, after enjoying the nice day with the family till about 9 pm, I had to rush to bed because I have to be up as early as 4 am to be able to make it to work at 5 am for the early morning Black Friday rush. While I am unable to enjoy most of the family time, the CEOs of the company get to spend time with their family; they get to travel to other states to visit other family members they haven't seen in a while. They can take a vacation during that time of the year, but I cannot because those days are blocked for workers like us. I have to be at work during the peak season. To make matters worse, while I am up at 4 am in the morning trying to catch a bus and a train, the CEO of the company is fast asleep snoring his or her heart out. I did this for five consecutive years and became fed up. So the question I asked myself again was, "How can one continue to do this thing for ten years, let alone twenty-five to fifty years?" and, "Is this why I came to this earth?"

As someone who is in a job position, you are the one that keeps the job going, but you are also the one that makes the smallest amount of money. **You help make the millions but never get the bonus** that comes from the millions you contributed to make. **You are tossed wherever you are needed** but not paid what you deserve or worth, but rather what they feel they have to give you. *You use your strength most of the time*. As a result of this one becomes very tired and is unable to do anything that will help benefit them.

Normally people who are stuck in the job phase spend more time partying and watching television because that's the only vision they have for themselves. Their primary focus becomes the new series on television or the hottest party happening around. Their mission is usually limited. **They need a new vision and focus** else they will be stuck in that position for a long time, if not the rest of their lives.

I looked at some companies' net worth and was fascinated at how much they are worth and how much they paid their employees. Some make about three hundred million dollars but pay their employees ten to twelve dollars an hour. Finally, from my study of people and my personal experience, I have noticed that people who work at a job are usually not happy with where they work. They might be happy the first couple of days they get the job, but that's as far as it goes. For those who are happy, they get stuck in the job phase and never move on. **Whenever you are in a job and are not happy, it is God letting you know it is time to leave the job phase. Make up your mind to move on first and then let your actions be evident of what you have in mind**.

Back to our teenager, they see that their parent is in a job phase and as a result, they also want to be there. If the parent does not envision something better for themselves, how will this teenager do any better unless a change is encountered some way somehow? However, the job they get is supposed to spark something within them to pursue greater things than to think of mediocrity. Let's look at some of our biblical figures.

We will be looking at three major individuals, namely Joseph, son of Jacob; and David, son of Jesse, and Moses, the brother of Aaron. Remember that your presence at every job brings about a blessing to that job place, in addition to you learning. This is because you make the flow of work go on. Being at a job is not bad, it helps you realize that you have true potential that has not yet been tapped into.

Joseph

So Joseph found favor in his sight and attended him, and he made him overseer of his house and put him in charge of all that he had. From the time that he made him overseer in his house and over all that he had, the Lord blessed the Egyptian's house for Joseph's sake; the blessing of the Lord was on all that he had, in house and field.

-- Genesis 39:4-5

One thing we can learn from Joseph is that every little child has a dream. If you were to ask any five year old what they will like to be in future, none of them will tell you "I want to work at a retail store." The very few who will say that are those whose parents themselves are stuck in a state of bondage. Every child wants to be something great. This is because God has built within every human, the ability to be great. As we continue in the other chapters, we will understand what God was doing.

From the story of Joseph, we know that he saw himself being in a position of leadership where his parents and siblings will be bowing down to him. This means that as a child he had a big dream of himself, but he would later be stuck in a prison cell. Sometimes circumstances will get us to a job, other times we, by ourselves, get ourselves there. Be it circumstance or ourselves, we should remember that that is not our position.

Joseph started off with a job as we see in the aforementioned scripture. Joseph was given the job to take care of the household of Potiphar, so he had to make sure the house was swept clean, all the water jars were filled and all that. He was using his strength at the time. This was good and dandy, but the potential he had was not realized, and as a result, this situation had to change. If we do not realize that the state we are in has to change, we will forever be stuck. ***Whenever God realizes that you are ready to leave your job, He causes a disruption in your job plans.*** Sometimes He will have you demoted, transferred or fired just so you can get out of your job. Joseph was now an overseer so, to say he was comfortable wouldn't be a wrong thing. God had to get him out of his comfort zone. When we read down the verses, we notice that his master's wife was making advances on him, which got him fired and moreover put in jail. When you are comfortable, God will shake up things around you. This quickens you and this is exactly what we saw in the life of Joseph. Though it wasn't his fault, he was moved from that comfort zone he was in. This lets us know not to get comfortable in our jobs.

David

Then Samuel said to Jesse, "Are all your sons here?" And he said, "There remains yet the youngest, but behold, he is keeping the sheep.' And Samuel said to Jesse, 'Send and get him, for we will not sit down till he comes here."

-- *1 Samuel 16:11*

David was not different from Joseph. David was supposed to be king of Israel. Whether he knew it or not, no one knows, but at a tender age, he found himself at a job he didn't care much for. He was a shepherd, always walking in the hot sun with a herd of sheep. Sometimes he had to fight off wild animals. He was employed by his father to take care of the sheep. If you know anything about David, you will understand that he was considered an outcast by his family, so taking care of the sheep was the only job he had. His father favored the other siblings more than him. The guy spent a lot of time doing a job. Because David didn't like the state he was in, he cried out to God for Him to save him as we can see in Psalm 69. Always smelling like sheep, having to feed them, he always spent his energy without impacting the lives of the sheep. The more he spent time there, he was encouraged to move on. Instead of ruling a nation, he was ruling over sheep. This is good because he was in a training stage for what was to come later on. Though he despised being with the sheep, he took the lessons and experiences seriously.

Moses

Moses was living in the palace of Pharaoh, king of Egypt, which many would consider to be a great position to be in. However, Moses thought otherwise. He knew he was supposed to be a deliverer, and as such, felt he was not in the right place. He was uncomfortable. This is another thing we learn from here—discomfort is a key to exit the job. He, however, learnt how to rule a nation while he was there.

Unlike David, Joseph and Moses who all had jobs but didn't consider their current state the final destination, some people get a job and consider it their final destination without thinking of moving forward. They actually pray that they do not get fired from the job, create a nest in that comfort zone and never learn to fly, let alone even fly. Whenever that happens, God shakes your nest loose to motivate you. You might get fired like Joseph, or you might be sent for like David, whereas others put themselves in a situation like Moses and have to run (See Exodus 2: 11-24). In all, make up your mind to leave your job and press on. A job is good for starters, but that should never be your permanent destination.

Even though it might seem like a job is not good, it has its importance and that is what we have to look at whenever we get a job instead of being stagnant or content.

Importance of a job
- ***It should motivate one to want to better themselves.***

At every job one gets to, you are supposed to be ***angered*** there. There are people sent there to upset you and to make your blood boil. Those people are there to make you question if you want to stay at that job forever. Sometimes they are coworkers, sometimes they are clients. They can even be your manager, boss or supervisor. I remember when I used to work at the retail store, one of my managers used to always work my patience. For some strange reason, he was the only person who was able to do that. The one thing I learned from that is that he not only helped me to manage my anger, he also motivated me to move from that place. Once that anger sets in, it is time to keep it moving. The anger is good and should motivate you to make progress in life, but not to act in retaliation against that anger. So, in my case, it made me pursue a career instead of maybe acting violently or speaking ill of that manager.

■ *It should motivate one to start a career.*
Some people may look down on you because of the education they think you do not have or the education they have attained. Others come in and, because of the money they make and their educational status, they think they are better than you are. These people also get on your nerves. They sometimes belittle you by lowering your self-worth. It is a propeller to push your life boat. Do not let that be an anchor that keeps you stationary. Whenever people look down on you, it is a signal that it is time to start packing. Do not complain when they do, rather, pick yourself up, have a vision and change your focus. They just motivated you to leave that job phase.

■ *It makes you question yourself.*
Every job is supposed to make you question your ability. It makes you think about what you are capable of pursuing as a skill. It makes you look at those who consider themselves managers and gives you the courage that you can do what they are doing, if not better than them. My wife had a job with a company she hated, yes hated. She was very much angered every time she even had to call the

office. Notice, I stated she was angered, this was the beginning of her questioning herself. She then told me one day, "these people do not even know how to do their career, I should be doing what they do, I will be better at it than they are". Eventually, she informed me that she wanted to pursue her MBA. That is the attitude a job is supposed to create in a person. ***Whenever hatred for a job settles in your heart, that is a red flag.*** One is supposed to envision a better thing for themselves than what their current position is. When you get to a point in life that you feel angered at the job you work at, it is the beginning of your breakthrough. Do not sit down, but rather break through. ***Have the attitude that you could do better than your supervisor.***

■ *God sets you up.*

You don't have to be a Christian for God to set you up, it is the principle that He has put in place. Once you are following that principle, He begins to set you up. He makes sure you get the job you want in the beginning stage. He just wants you to start the process. Once the process is started, He works through others to push you. He wants you to know that by your strength, you can never gain wealth. It takes something bigger than just working a job. Every money or income that comes your way will not sustain you as long as you continue to lean on your strength. Let's see if the next stage is a better choice than the current state we are in.

Recap

- *Whenever hatred for a job settles in your heart, that is a red flag*
- *The income from a job never sustains you*
- *You always strive to get more jobs to maintain the lifestyle you can barely manage*
- *Have the attitude that you could do better than your supervisor*
- *It should motivate one to want to better themselves*
- *It should motivate one to start a career*
- *It makes you question yourself: "Is this what I want to be doing for the rest of my life?"*
- *Whenever you make an effort to leave your job, God makes sure that He sends someone to help you out in ways you cannot fathom*
- *You help make the millions for companies but never get the bonus at this stage in life*
- *You are tossed wherever you are needed, but not paid what you deserve or worth,*

but rather what they feel they have to give you

- *You use your strength most of the time*
- *Whenever you are in a job and are not happy, it is God letting you know it is time to leave the job phase. Make up your mind to move on first and then let your actions be evident of what you have in mind*

Work hard. And have patience. Because no matter who you are, you're going to get hurt in your career and you have to be patient to get through the injuries.
-- Randy Johnson

2

CAREER

The blessing of the Lord makes rich, and he adds no sorrow with it.

-- Proverbs 10:22

The next thing on our list is the career phase. About fifty-five percent of young men and women around the world are in this phase. Forty percent, however, are in the job phase. As the years grow, more and more people will want to join this group, this is not a bad move though. The career phase has become the most common phase. Not long ago, it used to be the job phase, but not anymore. Many of us think the career we badly want will be the thing that will make us wealthy leave us feeling fulfilled. Is that true? Your job is supposed to help you to your career, but is your career the best fit for you as an individual? Very few are actually able to accomplish this.

One thing most people want when they get to the western world is this dream that some term "the American Dream". What is this American dream they talk about? This dream (I have come to understand) is this, going to school for at least four years to pile up student loans. After piling that student loan, you graduate with a degree that is supposed to propel you to work for a company you long and dreamt to work for, get married and settle down. Whenever people get out of college, they are eager to start working for a reputable firm. This may even be the same place they had a job, but fortunately, they no longer have to use their strength—they only need to apply the skill they acquired. After getting their career started, they continue with the pursuit of the American Dream by buying a house with a fifteen to thirty-year mortgage. Before we continue, let us even consider what a mortgage is. The root word for mortgage is "morgue", which stands for a place where corpses (dead bodies) are kept to be claimed, so this combined with "age" gives you "a dead body with time." This means once you get a mortgage, you live at the place waiting to be dead and claimed by your mortgage lender.

Several individuals after getting the career they want and the house they want, they feel accomplished because they have been able to get the middle class. This is where the problem lies. The middle-class syndrome, a lot of well-educated people are in this section of life. They are more focused on their career that they don't actually stop to think about what the middle class is all about. What is this middle class anyway? It is the position in life that keeps the rich, rich and the poor, poor. What do I mean by that? Well, with all the debts that have been piled up from the mortgages and student loans to car loans, a person in the middle class will be paying the interest monthly to keep the rich stable, whereas he or she can barely make ends meet. The banks keep taking the little money you make as a middle class and use it to pay the rich who lend you the money. I find it interesting however that people find that comfortable.

Furthermore, with the little income that one makes, the government taxes you and use that money to support people on welfare, most of which do not want to even get a job, though there are others who need that little help. You are stuck in the middle, helping keep both sides of the economic line stable whilst you are unstable in your own situation.

What then is a career? Is it good to have a career or not? Let us find out. A career is defined by the Merriam Webster dictionary as an occupation undertaken for a significant period of a person's life and with opportunities for progress. This is a very important definition of what a career is because it is the basis of everything we will be talking about. Whenever we make up our minds to pursue something as a career, we look forward to staying in that career for a significant amount of time while climbing the ladder to the top.

Most, if not all, of us look to work with the skills we acquired from school and work with one thought in mind, to retire with a good pension. When we first start our career, we are excited because we have joined the "working class" and think that all is well. After the first year of working with your skill you start to feel uneasy because you realized the money you make there is not enough and that with the experience you have gained, you can work elsewhere and make more than you are making presently. I have a friend that was in the same predicament, he knew the career path he wanted to embark on when he finished his education and started pursuing that career, and he was excited the first year. He used to always say he was not going to leave the place he worked because that's the career he longed for. After the first year, he started complaining about the same career, he wanted to pursue something else. To make it better, he wanted to leave the company he worked for. He had gained an experience that he thought will give him the ability to make more money elsewhere. Looking at the definition of what a career is, we can tell that this was what my friend was going through. He had a career that gave him the opportunity to grow, opportunity for progress.

We like the opportunity we get during our career phase, but we often take that opportunity because we think of the increase in monetary benefits. When it has no monetary benefit, we often let go of that opportunity. We often complain when such opportunities are presented to us, thinking we are being taken advantage of. Most of us pray for God to make us millionaires, but when God is taking them through the process, they start to complain. This is what the career phase is all about.

One thing I like to do is to ask people what they want to pursue as a career. Several people for instance, will answer nursing or computer scientist or software engineer. Rarely do you hear anyone say a comic or artist. My follow up question is usually, "why do you want to do that?" One thing I noticed that I find disheartening is the answer most people like to give. Some of these include, "the salary is great", "the benefits are unmeasurable", "because of job security." We always look at the career we want to pursue because of these and other things such as retirement and other benefits. I am not saying it is not necessary, but rather, let's look to learn something from the stage. All this happens because of the system we live in. For instance, the curriculum in schools is set up in such a way that you go to school to study a course that will help you come out to work for someone else. With this in mind, people only think about the money they will make with the knowledge they have acquired. Well, the career phase

> *Your career is like a box of chocolates - you never know what you're going to get. But everything you get is going to teach you something along the way and make you the person you are today.*
>
> *--Nick Carter*

is like the wilderness phase of freedom. It is at this stage that you are trained on the nitty gritty of business and management of things that belong to other people. You will learn many things at this phase, but what you learn might not bring you more income in the current phase. Because most people do not know what they are supposed to be doing at the career phase, they get stuck there and retire. After retirement, most of them die. Whenever people retire from their career, most of them still feel uneasy in their retirement, and as a result, they come back to work in the same career field, and sometimes the same company. People like that usually feel there is something still missing and think that going back to their career will help solve that. I had a coworker who was a math teacher. After several years of teaching, he retired. After about three months of being out of work, he came back, wanting to teach the same students he always complained about.

When you are in a career, you get promoted, but there is a limit to where you can reach, and then after a period of time you are considered, for a lack of a better word, "useless to the system", so you have to retire. When the companies have taken all they think you can offer, they send you packing with not even the same amount of money you were making before retirement. That is a sad thing. People who come to understand that career isn't the key to success usually try to break free. Whenever you try to break out from this, people say that it is not possible and that that is the only way to make it. However, it is normal for such to happen, but whenever people say that, it means the time is right. This is what usually causes a lot of mid-life crisis. People pursue a career they think will bring them money, but along the line, it seems like that career is not fulfilling their proposed dreams. With that in mind, many think they chose the wrong career and regret not choosing something else. Like the wilderness, the career phase is a training ground. This stage prepares you in several ways possible. It is at this stage that numerous opportunities arise. You can take up that prospect or let it slide, but as long as you are not ready to take that opportunity, you will forever stay in a career. For example, when I first started working in my career field, I was put on a cabinet team. As the other technology person there at the firm, I thought I should be out of the cabinet members because my supervisor was already on the team. I honestly didn't know why I was placed on the cabinet. We used to meet every week and I strongly believe it took me away from my work.

Whenever we were at the meeting, I honestly never said anything. Instead of paying attention to what was taking place, I just did my own thing. Little did I know that it was a training session for me. God always places us in a career to prepare us for our work. In that career, He makes sure certain opportunities are made available to us. These are what we will need to grasp on. In my case, I was getting introduced to organizing and managing meetings, taking feedbacks and learning the qualities of being a leader in that setting. Learning to handle the different emotions that rise up during a meeting and also how to contain them. With that said, I cannot stress enough about how important the career stage is—that is, it is a training ground. You get a career in a reputable company not so you can boast about it, but so you can learn the trades and way they work there. The money might be good, but that shouldn't be the focus, the focus should be what one is learning there. God then opens a way for you to find favor with someone in a high position who will make sure to push you closer and closer to people in influential places; sometimes God uses even your immediate supervisor to make this happen. But as that happens, you have to *make sure to learn anything that person is offering to impart to you*.

In this stage, you combine what you learned from the job phase and the acquired skill. The job phase makes you strong, whereas the career phase makes you think smart and quick. You learn to combine the two here. However, this is a point of stagnation also; many people get to this point and then get stuck. They become content, sometimes even purchasing more education just to help them stay in the same career, whereas they are not impacting any life. For instance, many people want to be nurses only because they believe the salary is good and the job security is very high. Because of that, they do not think about the impact they can have on others by exploring other ventures of nursing. They like to just work in a hospital setting but won't think about opening up their own practice in a neighborhood that urgently needs one.

We will talk more about such in the next chapter. We should get to a point where we are not comfortable working for someone. It is at this point that one should ask his or herself this question, **"Who am I impacting with this career? Is this why I came to this earth?", "Where is this career taking me?", "What am I learning from this career?", "Will I still have to do this?", "Will this make me wealthy, or will I have to get another venture to sustain me?", "What legacy am I leaving on this earth?" and the like.** When these questions start to flood your mind, it is the ultimate beginning of something extraordinary. This creates something I call, "holy fear" which terrifies you. A fear that makes it seem like you have to leave your current position. Nevertheless, make sure you do not rush to leave. Ensure that you have acquired all that you need to acquire at your current position. It is at this point that you start to find something I call your work or purpose, which will be discussed in the next chapter.

Finally, the career phase is the stage of challenges. These challenges **come to test your character** as to whether you will stay and continue to learn or give up. It is like the wilderness stage of freedom, so your character building becomes very important. As stated in my personal story, more responsibilities will be given to you, ones that actually do not correspond to your job, but take them on and do them with excitement. Let's take a look again at Joseph and David.

Joseph

And the keeper of the prison put Joseph in charge of all the prisoners who were in the prison. Whatever was done there, he was the one who did it. The keeper of the prison paid no attention to anything that was in Joseph's charge, because the Lord was with him. And whatever he did, the Lord made it succeed.

-- Genesis 37:22-23

Joseph moved from his job at Potiphar's house to the prison. Even though he was in prison, that didn't stop what he was capable of doing. He learned many things in Potiphar's house, including how to manage affairs. He used what he learned there when he got to prison to the point that the prison keeper put him in charge of all the prisoners. He was now in his career of overseeing the prisoners. While there, he learned how to manage affairs. He didn't only learn, but also saw other opportunities and made sure to grab those opportunities. When he was offered the position of supervisor in the prison, he didn't ask why he has to be the one doing that, but rather took the challenge and used it as a stepping stone. While there he did something that we all need to do(this will be tackled shortly). He used the gift he had freely. Like Joseph, *take every opportunity offered to you by your leaders in the career path, learn something at your current company or field for you will need it.* Even after helping out the butler and the cup bearer, they forgot about him (See Genesis 40). This will discourage most of us. Whatever happens in your career should not discourage, but rather motivate you. I know we are humans so discouragement will definitely come, but try to move past it as Joseph did. Do not focus on it, but keep your head high and do not be derailed by such things.

David

And David came to Saul and entered his service. And Saul loved him greatly, and he became his armor-bearer. And Saul sent to Jesse, saying, "Let David remain in my service, for he has found favor in my sight." And whenever the harmful spirit from God was upon Saul, David took the lyre and played it with his hand. So Saul was refreshed and was well, and the harmful spirit departed from him.

-- 1 Samuel 16:21-23

David had a job as a shepherd, taking care of his family's sheep. He had a skill of playing an instrument and with that skill, he got a career playing at a very reputable place—the king's palace.

While at the king's palace, he wasn't only playing, but he was learning the in-depths of being a king. He was studying what to do as a king and what not to do. He later got an opportunity to become the king's armor bearer. The more dedicated he was to his career, the more he learned. Even when Saul tried to kill him, he didn't let that discourage him from learning. Unlike David, most of us give up when challenges come. In his career, David was faced with several instances where even his life was in danger, but because of the lessons he was acquiring, he wasn't moved. The challenges he faced helped build his character. There were other instances that could have discouraged this young boy, but he never allowed that. He saw it as an opportunity to grow and took it. See every problem in the career field as an opportunity.

Moses

Moses fled to another place only to become a sheep herder. During that time he had to learn to manage stubborn animals and explore the wild wilderness. It was also here that he was able to hear the voice of God. He never complained about the terrains he was exploring or how the sheep were, but took his time to take in everything that experience had to offer him. With that, let us look at the purpose of a career.

Importance of a career
■ The urge to better yourself increases.

You start to question yourself and your ability especially when you realize that you are working more but getting paid little for all that you do. You become determined to be better than you are now. You are always moved to take on any open opportunity that you see available. Your ears and eyes are attentive for the slightest chance you see. Usually, when we see these opportunities, we think of monetary gains, but that should not be the case. When the drive for opportunities starts to increase, it is the root for great pursuit.

■ You aspire to be great.

At the career field, you are supposed to find someone who draws your interest, someone you aspire to be like. They motivate you to become a better you. They might either be older or younger than you. They come when the time is right. When you have learned all that you need to learn from the career stage, they immediately show up. They might say something that will get your mind thinking. They might even be people you have known for a very long time, but they will always wait for the right time to impart that word on you. These people are sent by God to let you know you have something great in you that has to come out. In the case of David, it was Jonathan; in Joseph's life, it was the butler who had even forgotten about him; and in Moses case, it was his father-in-law.

■ Finding your work

Once the inspirer comes in, they create in you an itch to start thinking. You either to think differently, or you start to re-examine your life to see if you are really doing what you were meant to do or you are just following a career path. Most at times, this is what causes that midlife crisis we talked about earlier because people notice that they have worked at a place for about twenty years and are still not happy. They realize they have wasted a whole lot of time, and start to regret. At this point you hear things like, "If only I knew what I should have been doing from the start." It is at this point that you find something I like to call *work,* which we will be discussing in the next chapter.

■ You meet your mentor

It is also in this phase that you meet your mentor. I will like to call this mentor your *"Elizabeth"*, while you are *"Mary"*. Elizabeth was pregnant with John the Baptist whereas Mary was just starting her pregnancy with Jesus (See Luke 1). Your mentor always makes the gift inside you become uneasy. Whatever you possess always makes your mentor's gift leap for joy because they can sense it. As a result, they motivate you to become who you are and not worry about the career.

In the career stage:

- You apply your acquired mental skills
- You learn to build character
- You are trained on how to manage other people's possessions, that way you will be able to manage what will be made yours
- You are taught to be responsible for everything you do
- You learn to be accountable to yourself and to others
- You learn the skills of and for the trade
- Your career has a time to it
  - o Your shift ends on the 24-hour clock
  - o Your period of employment ends at an age (55 and above)

Recap

- *When it has no monetary benefit, we often let go of that opportunity*
- *When you are in a career, you get promoted, but there is a limit you can reach and then after a period of time you are considered, for a lack of a better word "useless to the system", so you have to retire*
- *It is at this stage that numerous opportunities arise*
- *You have to make sure to learn anything that person is offering to impart to you*

- *A fear that makes it seem like you have to leave your current position, but at the same time, it terrifies you to leave*
- *Challenges come to test your character*
- *Take every opportunity offered to you by your leaders in the career path, learn something at your current company or field for you will need it*

We're here to put a dent in the universe. Otherwise why else even be here?
-- Steve Jobs

3

—

SOURCE OF WORK

The two most important days in your life are the day you are born and the day you find out why.

-- Mark Twain

After working at my career for about three years, I felt very uncomfortable. I loved my career when I first started, so what went wrong? I loved the fact that people will call me to fix their electronics. Whenever I woke up to go to the work place, I was not always filled with joy. I get there, I put a smile on people's faces but I just couldn't wait to leave there. "Is this what life will be all the time?" I asked myself. Will I be waking up every morning doing the same thing over and over, always a system of basic routines? I could not understand it. Is this what people have been doing for years? That was when it hit me that I was pursuing my career, but still couldn't make ends meet. I was not married, a single young man living at home with my parents but my money was not enough. I had no children, but I also had no money in my account. This career is not cutting it, life should be more than this. If my career is not cutting it both financially and emotionally there has to be something more. One day as I was giving counsel to a friend, I noticed that he was listening intensively. He then asked if he could record me while I spoke which ignorantly I complied to. As I was talking to him, he interrupted me and made this statement, *"**King**, I will pay to hear you speak, I feel every time you talk I have to record you"*. This was the wakeup call I needed. **I found my *work*.**

Have you found your work yet or are you still trying to maintain that career? So we know what a job and a career both are. What is work then? Work is defined as an activity involving mental or physical effort done in order to achieve a ***purpose***. That is one thing we have misunderstood for quite some time.

Some people think that work is a curse, especially most Christians. They think that praying and relaxing moves God to do work that He has given them. The Hebrew word for work is *abodah,* which literally means to "labor" or to "be of service". Usually we think of these as a negative thing, but in reality they are positive. When a woman is in labor, we notice that she tries to force what is in to come out, and that is what work is. Service is what we offer to people, so the two definitions work together—***bringing something within you out and serving it to others for them to benefit***. Let us dive a bit into this mystery— is work a curse or blessing? To start this off, let us first find out how we were created, this being our foundation and then we can build on this foundation.

> *Then God said, "Let us make man in our image, after our likeness. And let them have dominion over the fish of the sea and over the birds of the heavens and over the livestock and over all the earth and over every creeping thing that creeps on the earth."*
>
> *-- Genesis1:26*

To be able to understand anything, we always have to go to the source. To understand what we as human beings are supposed to do, we must understand where we came from. In the creation account, we notice that God created us after Himself, that is, in His image and His likeness. The image of God is a (Kingly) Spirit being as can be seen in John 4:24. He is also a good God. All these are *key* characteristics that we need to know about Him. His likeness is faithfulness and also a hard worker. Since we were created in the image and likeness of God, we bear the same nature as Him. This is why man is a spirit but he lives in a body of dust. Being that our real self is a spirit, we possess the same likeness as God. We are then supposed to be faithful creatures who should be hardworking. But is that the case? One thing God always did if you examine the creation account in Genesis is that He always states the purpose for creating that thing and then right after that He assigns it.

Usually, the purpose of the thing is built within it and that is what He expresses. The ability to accomplish it is also embedded in the nature of that thing. For instance, in creating the sun and moon, it states, *"And God said, Let there be lights in the firmament of the heaven to divide the day from the night; and let them be for signs, and for seasons, and for days, and years: And let them be for lights in the firmament of the heaven to give light upon the earth: and it was so."* (Genesis 1:14-15). In this scripture we see something that God did, He pronounced what He was creating by stating that let there be in the firmament. After, He stated the purpose for it by saying it will be for seasons and signs, for days and for years. Finally, He assigned the lights to the earth to shine on it. So to stress on it, God always has a purpose for creating something and also has an assignment for that thing. In the scripture concerning mankind, He stated our purpose and then assigned us the responsibility all in one. We were created to be like Him, that was our purpose, and our assignment was to have dominion over the whole earth. This is the work that God gave us. This was not a job that God intended for us, but rather our assignment and purpose.

As I stated earlier, we were created like God Himself and as such possess His nature. The first thing that describes God in the bible is something deep. The Bible introduces God firstly as a creator, meaning He is someone who is always working. He is not merely working, He works with a purpose behind it. What do I mean by that? Well, like any manufacturer, they have a purpose for creating something and also that creates in them the will to keep working. As a result of this, every human has in them the same will and desire to do something that will fulfill some type of purpose. This is what work is all about. When we look at the purpose for which God created mankind, we see our assignment being stated. This is what introduced the work we are supposed to be doing.

A lot of people think that work is a curse, but it is not. Just like the tree that is able to bear fruit, every human being also has to bear fruit. When I talk about fruit here, I do not mean precisely the fruit of the Holy Spirit, but rather the fruit that is hidden in us.

And on the seventh day, God finished his work that he had done, and he rested on the seventh day from all his work that he had done. So God blessed the seventh day and made it holy because on it God rested from all his work that he had done in creation.

-- Genesis2:2-3

First off we see that even God who is the creator of us all has His own work. Before we go on, let us see something that God did. The scripture says that He rested on the seventh day from all His work which He had done. Meaning at the time, the only work God was concerned about was the work of creation. His original work is that of a king, but he never rested from being a king. Rather, He rested from the work of creation.

To reiterate, the first way God is introduced to us in the bible is as a creator. If He is introduced as a creator, that makes that His work. The first thing we find out about trees is that they should bear the fruit of their kind, which was their work or purpose. As we saw earlier, the same goes for mankind, we were introduced as dominators, meaning there is something we ought to be dominating here on earth. The question is, are we doing it? Once we are able to do that, only then can we truly enjoy Sabbath. So, for instance, if you are supposed to dominate as a movie star, when you finish one movie, you can enjoy your Sabbath as you prepare for the next movie to dominate. Because mankind has been occupied with career, we miss out on the opportunity to dominate in the area God wants us.

How can one know their work?

When I was a child, I wanted to write books, I saw myself being a successful author. Down the line, I started writing novels in my school notebooks. I was a good artist also, but my passion was in writing. I enjoyed writing fictional stories and gave them to my friends to read. If any of them could recall now that will be great. Anyway, when I got to the sixth grade, I started listening to what people kept saying and because of that I wanted to be a medical doctor/surgeon. The fun fact was that I was someone who could not stand seeing blood. So I always wondered how I will fit in as a doctor. With that, I decided that I will become a pilot. Another fear factor kicked in, I was scared of height. I then went the easy way, I resolved to learn about computers. I convinced myself to think this way, "I am still a surgeon, maybe not on human beings, but on a computer. It's the same thing, except there's no blood". This made me think I was fulfilling my purpose of being a doctor. The mistake I did was this, I listened to what others were saying and wanted to pursue what they thought seemed right. One thing I applaud my parents for is that they never pushed me to do what they wanted as some parents do, but they gave me the room to be able to make decisions on my own.

Many children at a young and tender age have great ideas in their head. Some have big dreams, like being the next Nobel Prize winner to being the next big astronaut or the world's renowned physicist. Very few are able to push through, while others are discouraged mostly by either parents, friends or even siblings. When we see something great in a child, instead of encouraging them and helping them perfect it, some parents discourage it. You notice your child is good at talking about sport and watching sports, give him or her some time every week to watch it, listen to this child, they might be a sports analyst someday. Instead, we scream and yell at them. The work of a person is usually found in their gift. This means the talent a person has been blessed with. It is this gift that gives people the dreams they have as children. Most at times, your work also can be found in an extreme circumstance or tragedy. When something happens to you or a loved one, that can bring about what your work is. The reason being that if that tragedy didn't happen, you will stay in your comfort zone and never mature into your work. Most people complain when such experiences happen, but those experiences are usually the breakthrough point to their destiny.

Problems are great opportunities to explore your work. We will talk more about this in chapter four.

Children usually believe they can do anything, but as they grow up, doubt creeps in and society also influences them that they cannot be what they saw themselves as. To find what your work is, recall what you dreamt of being when you were a child. The one thing that gave you joy when you talked about it. That very thing is usually your work. See the thing with one's work is that it is fulfilling and comes with ease. You get joy out of doing that work. If you have something in mind that makes you happy and you feel it will be fulfilling, you are a step closer to finding your work, your purpose for existence. If whatever you are doing now is not fulfilling, that is not your work. At the outset of your work it usually doesn't pay, but with determination, it eventually pays off. When we look at God, He found it fulfilling to create, this is why whenever He finished something, He said it was good. *If whatever you are doing does not push you to say this is good, you should start rethinking and searching through yourself*.

For parents this is the key, whenever you hear your children saying they want to be something in the future, do not discourage them, but rather encourage them by investing in whatever they have in mind. If you see a gift in them also do not hesitate to push them up with any resource you have available.

My Father is working until now, and I am working.
-- Jesus Christ (John 5:17)

4

—

SUCCESS IN ONE'S WORK

Now that you've found your work, what do you do? I believe this is the reason why most people do not move from their career to their work. The question many people ask is this, "Ok I have found my work, what now?" I have come across many people who are in this stage of life. After several years of walking through life not knowing what their purpose on earth is, they finally find the purpose and are stuck. Some people even quit their career when they find their work but do not know what next to do. Out of frustration, they go back into the career field thinking that they made a mistake. This is normal, many of us have been there, and others are also on their way to that stage in life. Anyway, finding your work/purpose is the primary key to being successful. What is this work? We will take a look at what purpose is and from there we will look at the other things one needs to do to make it in our work.

Purpose:

The heart of the prudent getteth knowledge; and the ear of the wise seeketh knowledge. A man's gift maketh room for him and bringeth him before great men.

-- *Proverbs 18:15-16*

Perhaps one of my favorite passage of scripture and also the basis for everything I do. The text above doesn't only say a lot, but teaches us what we ought to focus on sharpening. Every human being here on planet earth was created with something in them that the world needs. There was something missing in the world and God knew that each individual had that thing in them and at the appropriate time it will come out. The sad thing is that every human being enters the world with what they have, but most leave the world with it without letting those alive benefit from it. God is a very purposeful being, in the sense that everything He creates, he did for a reason. One thing I have come to understand about this awesome creator is that whenever He creates something, He embeds in the thing the ability to fulfill its purpose. What do I mean by that? For instance, He created a tree and put that tree in a seed, so once you have a seed, it is easy to get back your tree. Whenever we see a seed, we know that the end result of it is a tree. Well, some of us also know that it has many purposes, such as providing humans with oxygen, food and other stuff, but inbuilt in that seed is the ability for it to become a tree under the right condition. God created mankind to be able to dominate in an area of talent.

Everyone has that one thing that they alone can do better. Others may do it, but it will be different. I often hear people saying there is no meaning to the lives they live, which is simply because they haven't found their purpose. ***Finding one's purpose then is the driving force to being successful. Success in itself is not what you have been able to accomplish as compared to others, it is being able to accomplish a part of your work.*** Purpose is the source of your work. It should be the driving force that wakes a person up. It is the reason for your existence and much attention must be given to it. Knowing your purpose alone isn't enough. Next, I will show us what we need to do after knowing what our work is.

Purpose creates a determination. People will discourage you once you find your work and are ready to pursue it. Regardless, finding your purpose always starts with finding your gift. If people discourage you, that shouldn't stop you, but that should assure you that you can actually do it. The more people say you cannot, it should be the driving force to push you. If people are not trying to discourage you from what you are trying to do, that might not be your work then. When you start having doubters, you are on your way to your work.

Perfect your gift

> *Practice is everything. This is often misquoted as practice makes perfect.*
> *-- Periander*

The statement "Practice makes perfect" applies to everything in life, including your gift. We have gifts and talent, but most of us think since it is a talent there is no need to work on it. Well, a seed is a tree, but it has to be watered periodically for it to first grow and then bear fruits. Finding ways to perfect your gift is very important. You want to make sure that whatever your gift is, you make it stand apart. Even if others are doing the same thing you do, yours is in a caliber by itself. For instance, if it is food you cook, you make sure that you find different ways to make your food taste better every time. Spend time with your gift, understand the essence of your gift and find ways to make it better and also seek advice on better ways to improve upon it. One thing that helps also with perfecting your gift is passion which we will talk about next.

Passion, Hunger, Thirst, Desire

Blessed are they which do hunger and thirst after righteousness: for they shall be filled.

-- Matthew 5:6

Passion is a great character that anyone who wants to be successful should aspire to have. Many people start a business, a ministry, a movement, but because of lack of passion for what they are pursuing, that thing never comes to see the light of day. I used to be the same way. I always start something but was not passionate about it. Once a little distraction comes my way, I stop and forget about it. Passion is the drive a person needs to move them in their purpose. First off, your purpose has set a vision for you, and to get to that vision you will need something to propel you there. That is when passion comes to play. What is passion then? It is defined by the Merriam Webster dictionary as, "a strong feeling of enthusiasm or excitement for something or about doing something". Let us take falling in love with someone for instance. Whenever the love is new, you want to always be around that person, you wake up thinking about that person and can't wait to even see them. That is what passion is all about, it is the urge to wake up and pursue something you love. Many of us lack this character. I call it the zeal to drive your purpose. Passion is what makes others see that you are ready for your work. Whatever you have a passion for it, it means you are ready to die for that thing. This also tells that what you think is your purpose is either your work or not. ***Your work is something you should be ever ready to die for***. If you are not willing to sacrifice all that you have to make your work a success, then there is no passion for that work.

> *Anything you do with passion is bound to attract people*
> *--Jemimah Sampong*

Your passion for your work will attract others. Jesus said "Blessed are those who hunger and thirst for righteousness: for they shall be filled", as we see in the text. Righteousness simply means right living. What is the right living here? The right thing that will propel you to accomplish your work.

Anyone who is eager and hungry to pursue the right living that will make them accomplish their work will definitely get that done. Many people are discouraged by family members that they will not be able to accomplish whatever they want to pursue and as a result, it kills their passion.

I quite remember hearing some of my friends arguing about passion and that passion doesn't get anyone anywhere. Of these friends though, most of them are working in their career and haven't been able to become the successful people they thought they will. Others, on the other hand, that are pursuing what they are passionate about are making it big. A good example of this is one of my friend who is a photographer. He never went to college but found his work early and started pursuing it. In his pursuit, he left home, but his parents couldn't encourage him. They kept telling him he couldn't accomplish what he had in mind. He found a job, got his first paycheck and bought a camera with that paycheck. With that first camera which cost him about $500.00, he was able to make about $2000.00. One thing he told me was that he was passionate about it so he kept pushing himself until one day he even got to take photos for a wedding which got him a high pay. To give an idea, he was paid about $50,000.00, not including the bill for the hotel space and car rentals for himself and his team. The one thing I got from him was that passion is important because it is that which helps wake you up to fulfill your purpose in your work. Again, passion gives you something to live and die for. If you want to just live day in and day out, you end up just wasting life, but when you have something to die for, then you are really living life.

Whenever your work becomes your passion, you do not need an alarm clock to wake you up, the drive to keep moving wakes you up every morning.

Planning

The plans of the heart belong to man, but the answer of the tongue is from the Lord.

-- Proverbs 16:1

Planning is one of the hardest things for many of us, and even I used to be poor at planning. However, it wasn't that I hated to plan, but that I didn't see the need to plan. I felt in life there was no need to plan anything, but rather to just flow with life. To be truthful, I thought that was faith, but that is totally wrong. For one to be able to show faith, they have to have some plan that they are looking forward to accomplishing. One thing most women are good at is planning, many men, on the other hand, do not take on this, but I haven't been able to figure out why. Most women, from my understanding, start planning their wedding as early as the age of twelve. But that is their wedding, what about their work? Before we talk about that, let us understand that planning is.

> *The secret of getting ahead is getting started.*
> *-- Mark Twain*

What is planning? It is identifying the goals or objectives to be achieved, and formulating strategies to achieve them. When you find your work, it always takes the planning phase to determine whether you will be able to make it or not. See, the planning shows what you see yourself working on in a time period. It is with that planning that you determine the structures and resources that will be needed. The planning stage helps you with the following:

- To set priorities
- Determine resources
- Set a time frame (to begin and finish)
- Be disciplined

Set priorities

Many of us do not know how to set priorities. Truth be told, this used to be me at a point in time. I never used to set priorities. Because of this habit, I became a habitual procrastinator. I did this while I was in the job phase. When I got to the career stage, it continued, but with much training I was able to learn how to prioritize. Also, since God wants all His children to find their work and accomplish it, He sends us to training as we saw in the other chapters. In our career phase, we are supposed to learn things like prioritization. Once we get to the planning phase, we are able to use the training here. When you plan then, you are able to determine what you should focus on first and what needs more attention. Because of lack of planning, we sometimes find it difficult to set priorities and this affects everything we do. Priorities are very important because they help you determine what needs to be accomplished now and later. It comes to play before the allocation of resources.

Determine resources

When you set right priorities, you are able to allocate every resource you have at your disposal well. They all work hand in hand. When your priorities are wrong, distribution of resources will also be wrong. You will end up giving more resources to a task that does not need them. Resources are not only limited to money, but include time and people, which we will talk more about down the line. When you plan, you are also able to figure out what you need to be able to accomplish your purpose. You are able to figure out the amount of work that is needed for you to put in each task.

Set a time frame

Time is the most important thing in the life of every individual who wants to be able to complete their work. Every human being has the same amount of time. The rich and poor, the sick and the strong, the one who has found their work and the one who hasn't, they all have twenty-four hours in a day. The way they allocate their time is what determines what they will be able to achieve. As stated before, time is a resource, and as such, must also be managed right. When planning, you are able to set a time to begin and a time you think you can set your work in motion. This should cover the time from beginning your work to the time it takes off. When you plan right, especially with respect to your time, you are able to discipline yourself very well. A key thing about planning then is discipline.

One thing to know about the human body is that it is a container of time. Every human body has an expiration on it, so living on this earth, one needs to allocate their time right in order for them to be able to accomplish their work on time before they depart. Many of us think we have all the time in the world to do waste, but if you are not able to accomplish your work on time, your expiry date will catch up to you before you know it. Time is just like money, besides there is an adage out there that states that, "time is money". If we know how to manage or allocate your money right, that same attitude should apply to your time. I see many people who take their money management very serious but are nonchalant about their time. The two need to be on the same level when it comes to allocation.

Be disciplined

If you plan everything right, the key thing then is to discipline yourself to be able to go along with the plan you have set. Discipline is the hardest part of the planning phase. Discipline, in my words, is setting standards and adhering to live by that standard without wavering or being moved by both external and internal forces. When you have done all the planning, you need discipline to be able to follow through with it. You can plan all you want, but if you do not commit to pulling through with it, it would be better if you hadn't started. ***When you are disciplined, you realize that time cannot be wasted***. It takes a change of mind to be able to discipline oneself. Setting standards for others to follow is easy, but when it comes to doing it to oneself, it is sometimes hard, but with a plan on paper and a daily review of it, one can be disciplined if one chooses to. It all comes down to a choice.

Finally, we always want to be successful in life. God has revealed to you what your work is. He has shown you the end, but it takes accepting that responsibility to be able to get to that destination. Once that responsibility is taken upon by us, we have to draw a road map and present it back to

God. With that plan in hand, it shows God that we are ready to embark on the journey. ***God has to see that you want to get to the end He showed you***. Your passion and planning are what gets you there. Planning is one thing many of us usually fail to do. It is best to have a plan, write it down and present it to God. Once

> *Plans are nothing; planning is everything.*
> *-- Dwight D. Eisenhower*

that is done see Him direct your path to your work, and if provisions are needed, He will supply them sometimes without you even asking Him. The aforementioned scripture lets us understand that planning is our part, once we do our end of the deal, then God is able to take care of His part. Once you are done planning and present it to God, He then gives the answer. Notice that it didn't say plan and make provisions yourself, but rather, that God has the answer to the tongue. So when all is said and done, write your plan and tell it to God and He will answer you with all that is needed to make your work possible.

Keys to Planning
- *Set your plan*
- *Write it down*

- *Speak it out to God*
- *Speak it out to others (not everyone will support or agree with you, that's fine)*
- *Be expectant on God's answer*
- *Make a move*
- *DO NOT RELAX, and*
- *Persevere*

Involve Others

And when he had called unto him his twelve disciples, he gave them power against unclean spirits, to cast them out, and to heal all manner of sickness and all manner of disease.

-- *Matthew 10:1*

A key thing to being successful is people. You can never do anything in this world without the help of others. We sometimes feel like we can do everything on our own, but that is not the case. You will always need people to help you get to your work. Better yet, you need people to help you while in your work also because they help keep it going. You can start alone, but along the way, you will definitely need others to push you. There are certain kinds of people you will need to help you get to where you are going. One way or the other, we have been in one of these positions in the lives of others who have found their work, so for us to get to our work, we will also need those people in our circle. These people include but are not limited to:

- The doubter
- The mentor
- The motivator, and
- The supporter

There are more, but to name a few, we will look only other the four listed. The others include the betrayer, the tester, the receiver, the quick tempered, the instigator, the analyst, the know it all, the mocker who is always ready to make fun of you when you are failing and has nothing else to offer, etc.

When I first wanted to pursue my work, I thought I could do it by myself. Little did I know that was all a joke. It gets to a point where you realize you can't do everything. If you have ever read my book, *"The mind, the tongue, our actions",* you will get a sense of the importance of people. Sometimes you do not try to involve people, but regardless, they come in as a result of the passion they see you possess. What I find interesting is that even Jesus who was fully God needed people in his ministry. Without the people He had, there would not be any ministry after his departure. He understood the power of involving others even though He was God. We can learn something from the people Jesus chose also. Take time to study the disciples of Jesus and learn to pick people like that in your inner circle. Let's take a look at the four people we listed before.

The doubter

This is the person who does not see beyond the present moment. They only live in the now and as a result, they believe you are limited to what you have at your current disposal. "Why bother to pursue your work?" is the question which is always on their mind. The reason you need people like that is because they give you a reason to prove them and yourself wrong. They are the people who make you want to finish your work right on time. The more you think about them, the more you have a reason to keep pressing on. These people make you discipline yourself in a way that you yourself wouldn't have been able to. They are the source of discipline. Do not be discouraged when these people doubt you and do not also push them away. Keep them around, the longer they stay around, the more you are pressured to get your work blooming. Most times, these people are people who are close to you. Their doubting you is not that they don't believe in you or your work, it is as a result of familiarity. Jesus had a doubter in His group also and he didn't push him away, but rather proved him wrong.

The mentor

This is the voice of advice and inspiration. A mentor is a very important person in the life of a pursuer. A mentor is someone you run to whenever you feel the work ahead of you is overwhelming. These are there to guide you in your path to life's fulfillment. Even if they do not believe in you or what you are pursuing, they are always available to impart what they know. They do not expect anything from you but are ever ready to give you the little information they have in store. You don't have to think about keeping them around because they are always there, they never leave until the right time comes. Even if they run, you will always find them. Remember, no matter what you know, you always need advice, even God the Supreme Creator of the universe listened to Moses' advice, how much more a mere human like us (See Deuteronomy 9:14-20). Remember, once your work is complete or even while you are working on it, you will be someone else's mentor. Lately, people look at certain celebrities and think they are mentors. The fact that someone has fame or status doesn't mean that they are fit to be a mentor. A mentor should be someone whose life is exemplary and also one that is able to offer sound instructions and advice when it comes to your work. Some mentors will actually discourage you. However, it is not the job of the mentor to be the doubter or the discourager, rather, they are to be the guide.

An advisor should also be someone you can easily go to with a problem and they are able to help you out without judging you. However, they are able to rebuke you. Their rebuke also should be taken as an advice or instruction. The mentor is that person whose opinion you value above others. They also help make you better than themselves. Anyone who is not seeking for you to be better than them is not a good fit for mentorship. They might be your discourager or doubter.

The supporter

The supporter is usually your biggest fan known to you. I will say this is the person who will support you even when you are failing only because they know that you are capable of doing something great. Others will not understand the purpose of this type of person. They are the ones who will sell you to others. This is somewhat your public relations person. When they hear people talking or doing something that relates your work, they are excited and want to share you with others. Such a person is needed; they help with networking.

Persistence
For a while he refused, but afterward, he said to himself, "Though I neither fear God nor respect man, yet because

*this widow keeps bothering me, I will give her justice so
that she will not beat me down by her continual coming."*
-- *Luke 18:4-5*

Do you give up easily? Are you easily
discouraged when things do not go the way you
expected it to go? Well, you are not the first to do
that, neither will you be the last. I was once like that
also. I used to always give up when my plans never
manifested like I envisioned it. This was not
because I didn't believe in what I had or what I was
doing, then I just didn't think there was any need
to keep pushing. The only way you can persist is
when you know where you are going and have a
passion. The driving force for persistence then is
passion. If you do not have a driving force
(passion) you can never persist. You cannot endure
when your plans are not going your way. To be able
to succeed, you need to possess a "can't quit"
attitude—this makes you successful. When you
have planned your work, sometimes it is hard when
you approach people to help you out.

Being resilient in your pursuit lets others
know that you are ready to move past your present
situation. The reason why some people make it in
life is not because they can do something, but
rather because of their ability to never give up.
Quitting too early is not the right attitude to have.
When people turn you down or do not believe in

your work, keep pushing till the right person comes along. When I started writing, not everyone believed in my work, some even thought it was just a hobby, but that did not stop me. When I became resilient in my pursuit, others saw the good in my work. Always persevere, especially when others are trying to bring you down.

Pursue Opportunity

And David said to the men who stood by him, "What shall be done for the man who kills this Philistine and takes away the reproach from Israel? For who is this uncircumcised Philistine, that he should defy the armies of the living God?"

-- *1 Samuel 17:26*

Opportunity is defined as a good chance for advancement or progress in something. Opportunity is something that everyone who is on the road to be successful in their work should look out for. There are endless possibilities and chances around us all the time. It takes one who is willing and looking for such opportunities to be able to grasp on to such possibilities. Whenever there's a problem, there is an open opportunity available; that opportunity might help with your work. What I have noticed is that many of us complain when a slight problem comes our way or we are going through something. Whenever something happens to us, it is an open opportunity either for us to advance or, in the case of someone else, to help them with their work. God does something strange sometimes, He causes a problem to usually come our way to help us get to an opportunity. But when such things happen we usually complain and miss out on the opportunity He was offering us. If you are ready to pursue your work you should be a walking opportunist, seeking and hoping to find an open possibility.

We sometimes look for big breaks thinking that that is the opportunity, but every small chance we get is ok, it is usually the small ones that lead to the big break. One thing also that helps with opportunities is a person's gift. As Proverbs 18:16 states, "A man's gift makes room for him and brings him before the great." It shows us that it is that which is within us that will create the opportunity for us. The very work that we are supposed to embark on is the same thing that will get us to where we ought to be. Your gift is also the very thing that is the source of your work. It is that then that can create an opportunity for you. Hence, working on your gift is very important. We will talk more about this in the upcoming sections.

It has been a while since we looked at David and Joseph so let's take a look at these young fellows again. One thing to remember is that sometimes opportunities come your way, other times you stumble upon it, while in some cases, you have to seek it out yourself. Either way, grasping hold of it is the key to unlocking your greatness.

David

In the aforementioned scripture, we see that there was a problem at hand. The Israelites were constantly being harassed and verbally abused by the Philistines and Goliath. This was a problem at hand, a problem none of them sought to solve. They instead complained and always withdrew from the problem until the young stud by the name of David came along. David saw a problem at hand, a problem no one, including the king, was ready to deal with. Understanding that a problem is an open opportunity, he sought to solve that problem, even if he had to use the wrong tools. Sometimes it is not about what tools you possess, but the self-confidence you have that you can solve the particular problem at hand. Even when you are unable to solve it, people appreciate your passion and desire to try to solve it. Let's learn something from the story of David and Goliath—the problem that will give you the opportunity to express your work is usually bigger than you and what you think you are capable of doing, but with determination and self-confidence, one is able to overcome that problem. In the case of David, he stumbled upon the opportunity. As stated before, sometimes you stumble upon opportunity, this is usually divinely orchestrated.

Joseph

Then Pharaoh sent and called Joseph, and they quickly brought him out of the pit. And when he had shaved himself and changed his clothes, he came in before Pharaoh.

-- Genesis 41:14

Attitude is very important when we get an opportunity. Even when we are in trouble and an opportunity arises, we should always have the right attitude. Joseph was locked up for something he didn't do and was wrongly accused. While being in jail, he used his gift to help some of his friends out of there thinking they will remember him when they got out but they didn't. Now if we are in Joseph's shoes, when Pharaoh himself called for Joseph, the first thing that will come to our mind will be "what have I done now?", but Joseph didn't have that attitude. When Pharaoh even told him about the dream, he didn't think about what had been done to him previously, but was focused on the opportunity he had been given to exhibit what he had in himself. He didn't stumble on the opportunity, but the opportunity was given to him to prove himself and he did. This is the thing about this kind of opportunity, those who give it to you know what you have, but they give you room to exhibit what you have within you, to see if you have the self-confidence. Many of us are given such opportunities several times but we miss it because we are not prepared. With such chances, one has to be ever ready to take them on when they arrive, else it holds one back from accomplishing or moving on with their work. Joseph was ready. Because of his readiness, he didn't think about past issues, but focused on the task at hand.

Opportunity
- Sets the stage for greatness
- Brings you before those who will help with your greatness
- Displays what you have within you
- Showcases your talents and gift(s), as well as your character

Pray/Seek the Lord's Direction
In all your ways acknowledge him, and he will make straight your paths.

-- *Proverbs 3:6*

The one thing that sets believers apart from the world is their ability to pray. Many Christians are religious with prayer to the point that they do not see the necessity of doing it. When someone in the world pursues their work they are able to accomplish it with ease, but when a Christian is able to pray while pursuing their work, they get an upper hand. Prayer is one thing that gives God the ability to help you with that work. When you find your work, you need directions to be able to go about everything you are doing. Many at times we rush with our work, thinking it is time for us to embark on that journey, whereas, in the eyes of God, it is not time yet. Whenever we seek God's directions, we are able to make conscious decisions which will help us down the line. After all the planning has been done and everything has been taken care of, this is the part that those in the world miss out.

When we look at Proverbs 16:1, it states, "The plans of the heart belong to man, but the answer of the tongue is from the Lord." This scripture says a lot. It lets us know that the planning aspect of our work belongs to us. Thus, we have to determine what we think we might need, do all the work and then present it to Him. The scripture states that the answer of the tongue belongs to God. What is that supposed to mean? Well, once you have finished planning and writing it down, you have to speak it out to the Lord. When you speak it out to Him, you let Him know that you are ready to embark on the journey. Speaking involves the tongue, so once He hears that, He gives you the provisions for that work. This way, everything you placed in your plan will be coming to life. If you put people, He will bring people who will help; if you wanted money, and time, He will help with those and you can allocate and assign as required. You become the manager of the work and a steward of the provisions.

Prayer is very important; it is through prayer that more ideas that can help with your work can be attained. Moreover, this shouldn't be a one-time thing, constant communication with God is vital. Since He is making the provision, He becomes a partner to help with your work, so it is important to keep Him in the loop of things.

Offer your work!

In America, we are told that nothing is free and that you have to pay a price for it. Well, when it comes to your gift you have to pay the price for it, but the price you pay is that you start by offering your work for free. Many of us do not know how to do this because we feel we have worked hard and because of that people should just be willing and ready to pay for what we have. Offering your work for free is a good way to get yourself out there.

When it comes to offering it freely, it shouldn't be to people you already know only, but to those you do not know as well. As a matter of fact, it is best to offer it to people you barely know. With people you know, they tend to support you for that very moment and then it ends there, however, people who do not know you who benefit from what you gave to them freely are always ready to push you up whenever the opportunity to do so comes. My gift, for instance, is to talk to people, to give sound instructions and to teach the Word of God. Whenever the opportunity presented itself, I did what I was supposed to do freely. If I visit a place and I see that someone there needed to hear something that I had to offer, I didn't hesitate to give it out freely. The same even goes for my books, whenever I see someone who can benefit from one of my books I sometimes give it to them freely. This helps with networking. It is through this network that people get to know who you are and are able to appreciate what you have worked out of your inner being. When we look at the account of Joseph in Genesis 41, we see him presenting his work freely to Pharaoh. Knowing that he was someone who could interpret dreams, he didn't say what we normally say these days, "what will I get from it?', "how much is he paying me for it". Rather, he offered it freely. The same thing happened to Daniel the prophet (See Daniel 2) where the king even offered to pay him for what he had but he refused and offered it freely. When he was done presenting, the king even exalted him. Let us learn from these two examples. Offer your gift/work/talent freely, it gets you out there even easier than having people pay for it will.

Recap

- *Finding one's purpose then is the driving force to being successful. Success in itself is not what you have been able to accomplish as compared to others. It is being able to accomplish a part of your work*
- *Your work is something you should be ever ready to die for.*
- *Spend time with your gift, understand the essence of your gift and find ways to make it better and seek advice on better ways to improve upon it*
- *Whenever your work becomes your passion, you do not need an alarm clock to wake you up, the drive to keep moving wakes you up every morning*
- *Planning helps you to set priorities*
- *Planning helps you determine resources*
- *Planning helps you set a time frame (to begin and finish)*
- *Planning helps you to be disciplined*
- *When you are disciplined, you realize that time cannot be wasted*

- *Time is the most important thing in the life of every individual who wants to be able to complete their work*
- *Being resilient in your pursuit lets others know that you are ready to move past your present situation*

Finally, one thing people fail at is learning how to market their work well. I had a similar problem when I started writing. Having done all this work, it takes a person willing to push their work out there. There may be opportunities, but if you do not take advantage of those opportunities, no one can help you. Marketing can come in many forms, but the best way is by getting your hands dirty. You might have to offer the work for free as stated before, but in doing so you sell yourself out there for people who know nothing about you or your work.

For I am already being poured out
like a drink offering, and the time for
my departure is near.
-- Saul of Tarsus (2 Timothy 4:6)

5

DONE?

And this was why the Jews were persecuting Jesus, because he was doing these things on the Sabbath. But Jesus answered them, "My Father is working until now, and I am working".

-- John 5:16-17

Many people start working and all they can think about is retirement. Whenever that is your motivation, you haven't entered into the work stage, you are either in the career or job phase. With a job, you are always looking to move to another job or get a career. When you are in the career stage, you are looking forward to retirement. All you think about is your pension or 401k, how much you can accumulate and how many years you have to go. That is the difference between the career stage and the work stage. In the work stage, there is nothing like retirement, as a matter of fact, you leave this earth while doing your work. Most people in the career phase want to get their satisfaction from their retirement. When you get to the work phase, your satisfaction comes from knowing that you have work to do and the need to accomplish that work.

People want to enjoy Sabbath all the time without even understanding the purpose of the Sabbath. They think retirement ends it all. I, for one, used to think God stopped working after creation, but in Genesis 2:1-3 it states,

> *Thus the heavens and the earth were finished, and all the host of them. And on the seventh day, God finished his work that he had done, and he rested on the seventh day from all his work that he had done. So God blessed the seventh day and made it holy because on it God rested from all his work that he had done in creation.*

We noticed that he rested from His work of creation which He was done with. This is to tell us that our work never stops, we finish a phase of our work and then we have to move to another aspect of our work. There is therefore different projects in each person's work. This means that once you are done with one project of your work, you take time to reflect on what has been accomplished and prepare to move to the next project of your work. For instance, if you are a musician, once you have produced an album, you do not retire, you rest and prepare for the next album or song. Jesus understood this and understood His father, which was why He stated in John 5 that His father is always working, and as such He has to also work. Like God, we never finish our work, unless our purpose on this earth is done. Jesus never thought about a day off or even retirement. He was always moving, accomplishing what He was sent here to do. That is the attitude we ought to have, focusing on achieving our GOAL. With that mentality, we realize that no time should be wasted and that every minute of the day matters.

For emphasis, we are all ambassadors sent to this earth to accomplish a mission. As long as an ambassador is in a territory, his or her work continues. When the work assigned to them is completed, they do not retire, but are called back to the home country. So then everyone has a time set for them to complete their work here. But to be able to finish on time is also very important.

Recap.

- *There is no retirement in your work, so avoid thinking this way. Rather, focus on finishing your work*

- *You make your schedule, meaning you either do not get to sleep much or you do not focus on sleeping. Your work keeps you up and it is the same thing that wakes you up*
- *You become a servant to others, especially to those who benefit from it. This is not a bad thing, but rather, you are always working to be able to meet the needs of people who rely very much on what you have to offer them. This makes you a leader. In the words of Jesus, "He who wants to be great must serve"*
- *You tend to feel that there is not enough time in the day, especially when tasks concerning your work are not complete*
- *Your priorities are different, no focus is placed on a pension, but rather the focus is placed on finishing what was started*
- *When all is said and done, you feel accomplished, you are a success and you enjoy the fruit thereof*

IMPORTANT

The Hebrew word, "*abad*" means work and when used as a verb, means "worship" or "to serve". This is the same word used in the Genesis 2:5. Your work is a sign of your worship to God, so whether you are a believer or not, as long as you are doing your work, you are fulfilling your purpose, and if you are fulfilling your purpose, you are worshiping Him. God is a king, and doing the bidding of a king is very important.

Whenever one does the will of a king, they express their worship to the king. To be here on this earth is the will of the king, and to do that which He sent you here to do becomes your worship then to him. Work and worship both have the same root word which is "wor". The root word is worth, worth in the sense that your work, for one, is something that is worthy of you, something that is deeply embedded in you. As such, the work you do brings about your worth for others to appreciate. So whenever you are fulfilling your work, people pay you what you are actually worth and not what they feel they need to give to you. Hence, if you are doing your work well and put a high price tag on it, people will still pay for it because that is your worth. In a job or career, however, others determine what you are worth to them and they end up putting a price tag on you. For your worship to God, it is what He's worth to you that you give to him. As a result, what is due Him is first off fulfilling the purpose for which He created you. When you are fulfilling what you were created to be, you are honoring Him as a Lord, hence your worship. See, whenever God creates something, He embeds in it the ability for it to fulfill its purpose so that it can give Him glory. When the sun shines or the moon gives its radiance, it is signifying its worship to God. But the moon and the sun are not really doing anything but fulfilling their work. When a mango seed is able to grow and become a tree, it waves its branches to signify its worship to God. The same goes to us as human beings. When we understand that our work is our worship to God, we will be eager to find it and fulfill it.

Your highest form of worship is doing what God created you to come here on earth to do. Once you are fulfilling His purpose and your purpose, you are offering Him a sweet savoring sacrifice.

Whenever you find yourself on the side of the majority, it is time to pause and reflect.

-- Mark Twain

Summary

Laziness has become the order of the day to a point where many people do not want to engage in any work, but they want to enjoy the benefit derived from hard work. Many people are looking to win the lottery so they can relax and do nothing because they feel that is the good life. Was man made to work or relax? Is work a blessing or a curse? We sometimes think that work is a curse, which is why we struggle to do it.

"Work: Is it a curse or a blessing?" deals with the three things we often interchange, "a job, a career and your work". David describes all three and teaches the benefits of all three and what one is expected to do at each phase. He finally talks about what work is and how one can find their work and pursue it.